WITHDRAWN

All aboard!

*To Sylvia Boorstein for teaching me Metta Meditation,
and my mantra, at Spirit Rock Meditation Center.*
—S.B.K.

♾This edition is printed on acid-free paper
that meets the American National Standards
Institute Z39.48 Standard.
♻Shambhala Publications makes every
effort to print on recycled paper.
For more information please visit www.shambhala.com.

Bala Kids is distributed worldwide
by Penguin Random House, Inc.,
and its subsidiaries.

Designed by Kara Plikaitis

Bala Kids
An imprint of Shambhala Publications, Inc.
4720 Walnut Street
Boulder, Colorado 80301
www.shambhala.com

Text ©2020 by Susan B. Katz
Illustrations ©2020 by Anait Semirdzhyan

9 8 7 6 5 4 3 2

Printed in China

Library of Congress Cataloging-in-Publication Data
Names: Katz, Susan B., 1971– author.
Title: Meditation station / Susan B. Katz.
Description: Boulder, Colorado: Bala Kids, [2020]
Identifiers: LCCN 2019006885 | ISBN 9781611807912
(hardcover: alk. paper)
Subjects: LCSH: Meditation—Juvenile literature. |
Mindfulness (Psychology)—Juvenile literature.
Classification: LCC BF637.M4 K28 2020 |
DDC 158.1/28—dc23
LC record available at https://lccn.loc.gov/2019006885

MEDITATION STATION

Susan B. Katz

Illustrated by
Anait Semirdzhyan

bala kids

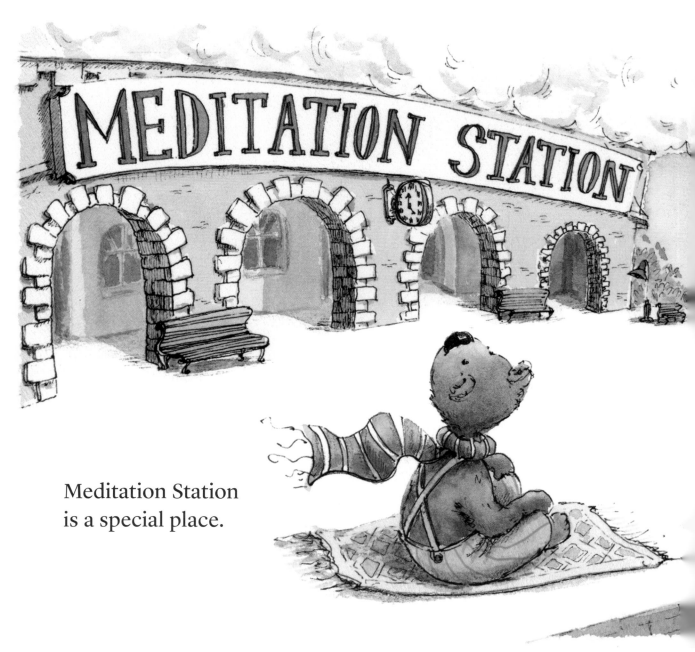

Meditation Station
is a special place.

Trains come
and go at a
speedy pace.

Thoughts are like trains
that zoom right by.

"What's that over there?"
"Wow! Can I try?"

Toot! Toot!

The conductor pulls a cord.

Chug-a-chug, choo choo!

"All aboard!"

Breathe in, wave to the engineer
in striped jean overalls.

Breathe out, smile as the caboose
passes and dispatch calls.

Whoosh

goes your breath like the
whistle's hot steam.

Listen as steel locomotives
squeak and scream.

Watch your train of thoughts roll down the railroad track.

Sit still and listen to the *clickety - clack*.

Wonder what's loaded in the wagons and cars?

Maybe magical potions or bright shooting stars

Look! It's a flatbed full of things you wish you could do,

like have birthday cake for breakfast or fly to the zoo.

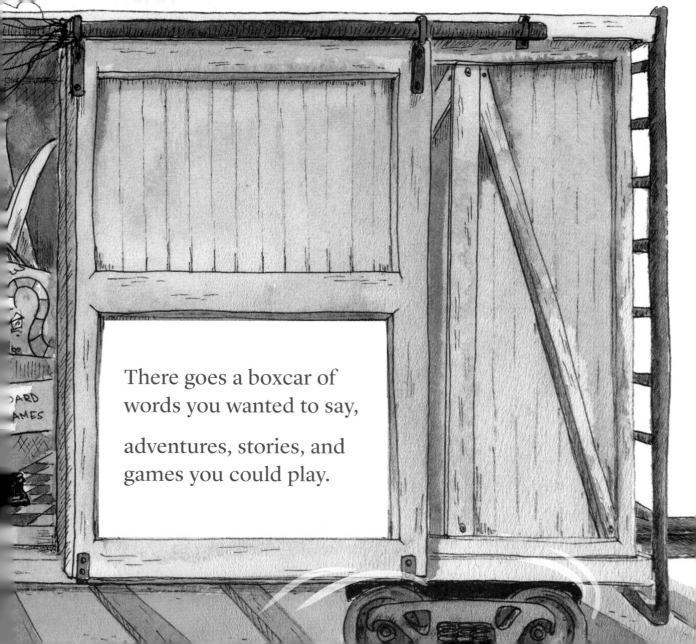

There goes a boxcar of words you wanted to say,

adventures, stories, and games you could play.

Wait! The signal lights are flashing: red, yellow, green.

stop and slow down your breathing machine.

Feel the *thumpety-thump* of your little heartbeat

from the top of your head
to the tips of your feet.

Inbound: a double-decker
diesel line.

Hear the hum of your breath
and you'll be just fine.

On the platform, no baggage,
is the perfect location.

Relax and enjoy
the Meditation Station.

MEDITATION

You can lie down flat
or sit crisscross.

Remember *you* are your own breathing boss.

As thoughts Zoom
in and out of your brain,

stay in the station and just
watch each train.

Susan B. Katz is an award-winning and Spanish bilingual author, National Board Certified Teacher, educational consultant, and keynote speaker. She has published several children's picture books, including: *ABC, Baby Me!*; *My Mama Earth*; *ABC School's for Me*; and *All Year Round*, which she translated into Spanish as *Un Año Redondo*. She has also written several chapter book biographies. Susan is the Executive Director of ConnectingAuthors.org, a national non-profit bringing children's book authors and illustrators into schools. Susan has been practicing metta meditation for over twenty years and regularly attends Spirit Rock retreats. When she's not writing, Susan enjoys traveling, salsa dancing, and spending time at the beach. You can find out more about her books and school visits at: www.SusanKatzBooks.com.

Anait Semirdzhyan is an illustrator who finds her peace of mind in creating children's book art by using traditional media, ink, and watercolor. When not working she also enjoys yoga and walking outside. Anait resides in the suburbs of the Emerald City—Seattle—with her husband, twin daughters, and a shaggy labradoodle. Visit her at www.anaitsart.com.